Discovering Electricity

Written by Rae Bains

Illustrated by Joel Snyder

Troll Associates

Library of Congress Cataloging in Publication Data

Bains, Rae.
    Discovering electricity.

    Summary: A brief discussion of what electricity
is, where it comes from, and how it is used.
    1. Electricity—Juvenile literature.
[1. Electricity]   I. Snyder, Joel.   II. Title.
QC527.2.B36   537   81-3339
ISBN 0-89375-564-8   AACR2
ISBN 0-89375-565-6 (pbk.)

10   9   8   7   6   5   4   3   2   1

Look around your house. Just about everywhere you look, electricity is at work. It makes light bulbs glow. It makes radios and TV sets play. It runs washing machines and refrigerators.

Electricity is working outside your home, too. It makes street lights shine at night. It makes traffic lights turn green and red.

What is electricity? Electricity is a kind of energy. It gives us heat, light, and power. But electricity is not a thing—like a dog or a mountain or a tree. Electricity is an action—like running or flying or swimming. You cannot see electricity, but you can see a clock running on electricity.

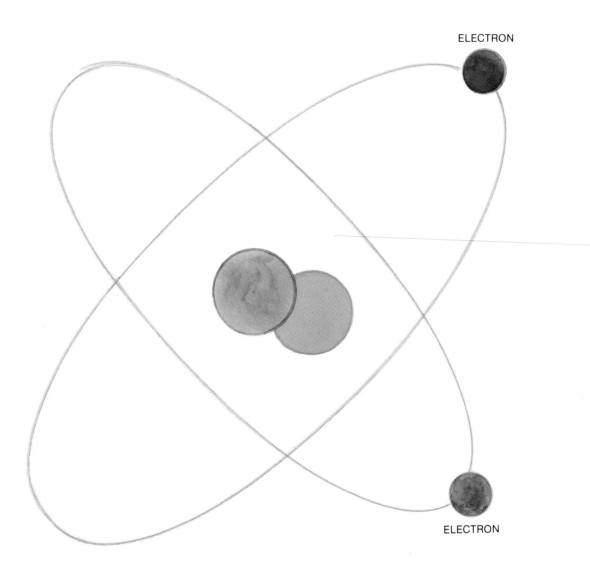

ELECTRON

ELECTRON

The things that make electricity work are atoms. Atoms are so small that millions and millions of them will fit on the head of a pin. Everything in the world is made of atoms.

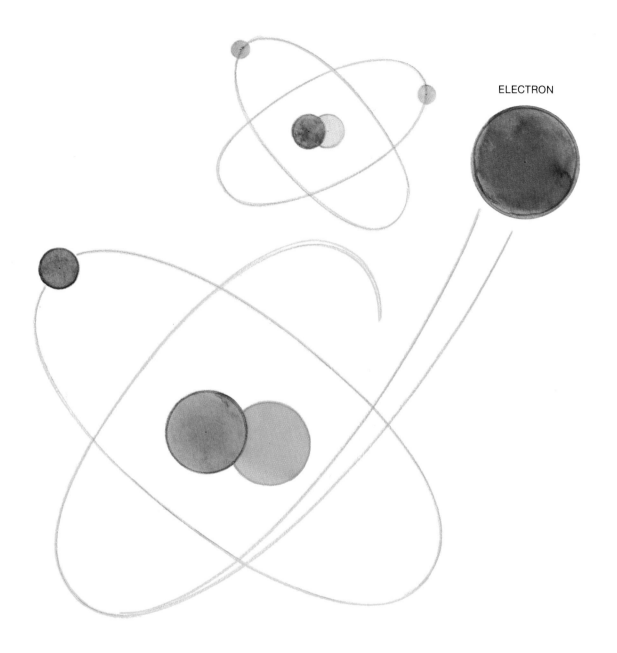

ELECTRON

Sometimes a bit of atom, called an *electron*, goes flying off. It joins another atom. That action—the electron flying from one atom to another—is electricity.

You make electricity every time you run a comb through your hair. You may hear a crackling sound. Some of your hair may stand straight up. You are hearing and seeing signs of electricity. The rubbing of the comb makes electrons jump. They jump from your hair to the comb.

The electricity you make by running a comb through your hair is a very tiny amount. It is not strong enough to run even the smallest machine. Many, many moving electrons are needed to light just one small bulb.

Even if you could make many electrons jump with a comb, you could not use them for anything. That is because the electricity made this way jumps in all directions. The electrons fly around like feathers in a pillow fight.

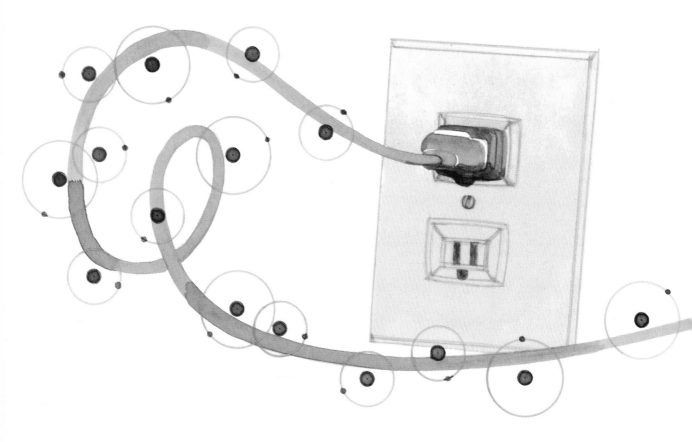

To use electricity, we must make it go where we need it. We do that by sending electricity through wires. Your TV set has a wire that is plugged into a wall socket. That wire carries electricity into the TV to make it work.

Wires carry electricity the same way pipes carry water. When we want water, we turn on a faucet, and the water runs into a glass. When we want electricity, we switch it on. Then it runs through a wire into a TV set, a lamp, or an electric drill.

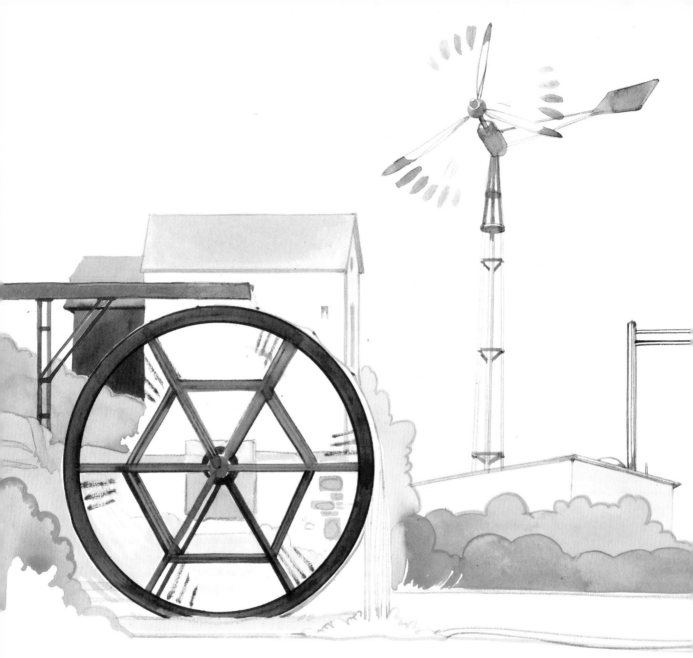

A water wheel turns when it is pushed by a steady stream of water. A few drops of water hitting the wheel will not move it. A windmill turns when a steady wind pushes it. Short gusts of wind will not keep it moving. Electricity—like water and wind—must flow steadily to do its job. A steady flow of electricity is called a *current*.

Along the streets of almost every town, there are tall wooden poles with heavy wires between them. The wires carry powerful electrical current. The wires—power lines—are far above the ground for safety.

Where does the electricity in these power lines come from? It comes from a factory called a power plant. There are huge machines called *generators* in the power plant. These generators make the electricity we need. This electricity is sent through wires from the power plant to factories, schools, stores, and houses.

Some machines need a lot of electricity to make them work. Other machines do not need much electricity. A flashlight that runs on batteries uses only a little electricity. The battery gives it all the power it needs. A battery is really a very small electrical generator.

A battery makes electrons. They build up on the metal inside the battery. The electrons are ready to give off electricity. You can put these electrons to work in a flashlight or in a radio or toy that uses a battery.

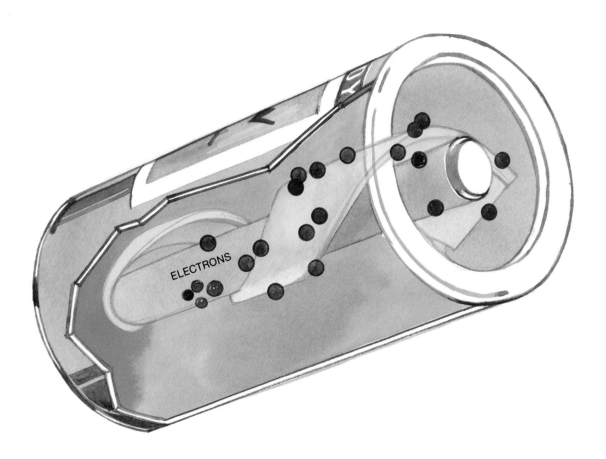

ELECTRONS

How do the electrons do their work? They make electricity by moving on a path called a circuit. A circuit is a kind of circle. When a group of children all join hands to make a circle, they are making a circuit.

To use the battery's electrons in a flashlight, we must make an electrical circuit. This circuit will carry the electrons from the battery to the bulb. It will make the electric light bulb glow.

When you press the flashlight switch on, you make an electrical circuit. The switch is like the last two children who join hands to close the circle.

Now, electrons move from the battery to a strip of metal inside the flashlight case. The strip of metal carries the electrons to the bottom of the little bulb.

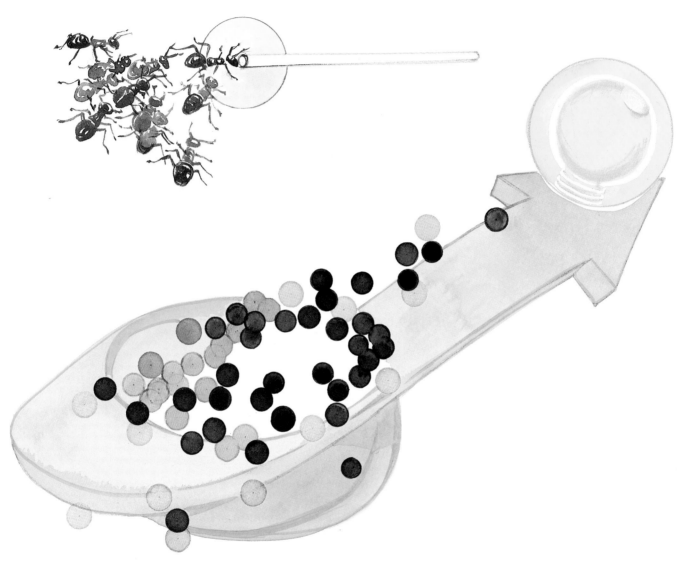

The wire inside the glass bulb is thinner than a hair on your head. When the flashlight switch is on, millions of electrons try to get into the bulb's wire at the same time. It is as if hundreds of ants were trying to squeeze into a drinking straw all at once. And they cannot stop trying, because hundreds of other ants are pushing behind them.

The electrons bang and push and rub against each other in the wire. This makes the wire hotter and hotter. The wire gets red hot. Then it gets white hot and gives off a glow. We call that glow "light."

The current of electrons will flow around and around the circuit as long as the switch is on.

When you turn off the switch, the circuit is broken. The flow of electrons stops, and the bulb stops glowing.

A flashlight battery makes a small amount of electricity.
The lightning flashing in the sky on a stormy day is a huge
amount of electricity. It is made by clouds rubbing against each
other. The electricity in a lightning bolt can make the night sky
as bright as day.

You can make a tiny bolt of electricity. Rub your shoes on a rug a few times. Now, walk to a metal doorknob. Point a finger at the doorknob. When your finger is very close to the knob, you will see a tiny spark. It jumps from your finger to the knob. You may also feel a tiny shock. A lightning bolt is millions of times larger than that.

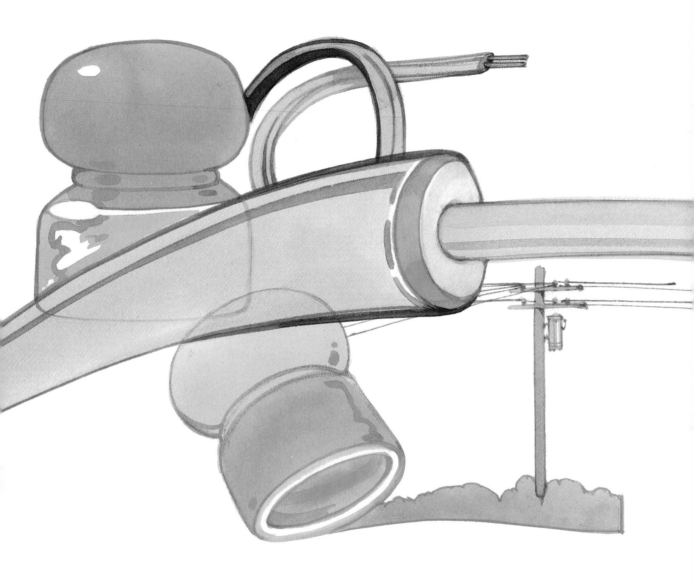

Electricity does many good things for us. But it can also do harm, if we are not careful. That is why electric wires are covered. The covering is called *insulation*.

Rubber is a good insulator. Electric wires are covered with rubber. It keeps the electric current in the wire, so it will not leak out and hurt us or start a fire. Other good insulators are glass, plastic, and dry wood.

Metal is not a good insulator. Most metals are good *conductors*. That is why metal wire is used to conduct, or carry, electrical current.

Water is also a very good conductor of electricity. This is why it is not safe to swim during an electrical storm.

Gases can also be very good conductors of electricity. Many lighted signs in store windows are made of glass tubes. The tubes are filled with gas. One kind of gas will glow red when electricity flows through the tube. Other kinds of gas will make the tube glow blue or yellow or green.

The conductor we use most often is metal wire. A very thick wire brings electricity into your house. It runs through a machine called a meter. The meter measures how much electricity is used in your house.

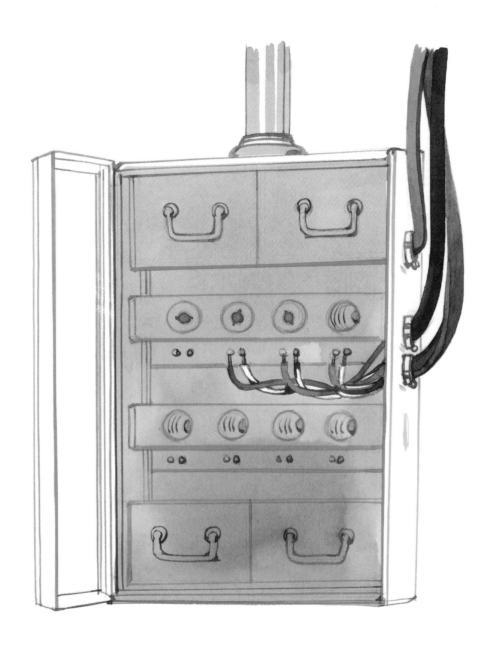

After it leaves the meter, the electricity runs into a metal box. In the box, there are circuit breakers or fuses. Circuit breakers and fuses are electrical "traffic cops." If too much electricity tries to get into a wire, a fuse stops it.

Wire circuits go from the fuse box to all parts of your house. One of the circuits goes into the kitchen. It brings electricity to the light bulbs. It also brings power to the sockets in the kitchen walls. The refrigerator is plugged into a wall socket, and so is the toaster.

What happens if an electric iron, an electric radio, and an electric mixer are added to that same circuit—and everything is turned on at once? It may be too much electricity for the circuit to handle safely. A wire in the fuse melts, and everything on the circuit stops working.

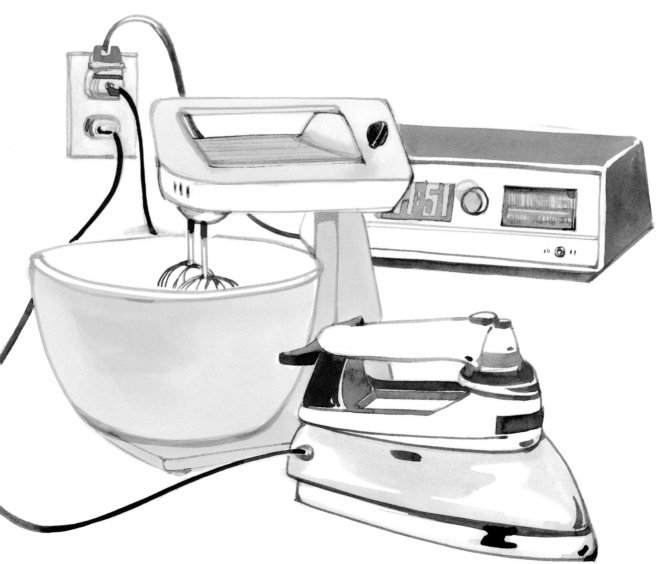

Too many electrons are pushing into the circuit. That could start a fire. So, the wire in the fuse does its job of being a traffic cop. It stops the flow of electrons into the kitchen.

Electricity runs the clock that wakes you in the morning, and the telephone you talk on. It runs the phonograph that plays your records, and it runs the life-saving machines in hospitals. Electricity performs its magic in many ways—it serves the whole world every second of every day.